The Learn How Coloring Book for Adults

Anti Stress Coloring with Knitting and Crocheting Tips for Beginners

Test page at end of book

Published By
RW Squared Media

Use all of your resources. Your local library probably has books, magazines and even videos to help you learn. Some may be available online.

Use the internet to your advantage. There are several good blogs to help you. Craftsy.com even has a free knitting class available online.

As valuable as the internet is, nothing beats talking to a friend. Use a friend that knits as a resource. If none of your friends knit/crochet, joint a stitch group.

Be careful using acrylic yarn. It may it separate or slip on the needle.

For a purl stitch, working yarn should be in front of your knitting.

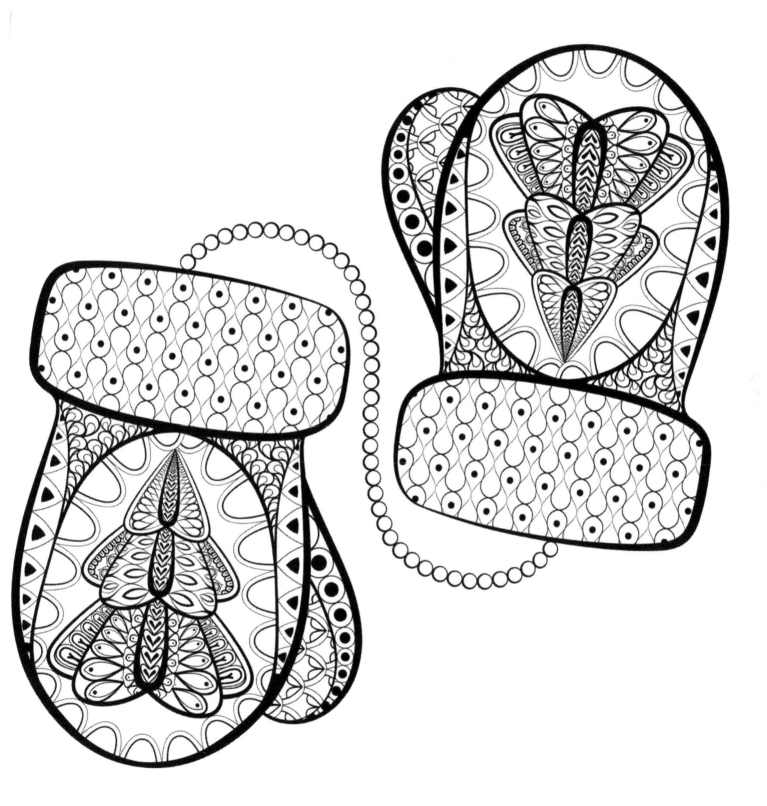

Understanding knitting gauge is crucial. Do your research and make sure you understand. A little investment here will pay huge dividends in the future.

For a knit stitch, working yarn should be behind both needles.

Use a row counter so you can always resume at the proper place. Don't have a row counter, use a pencil and paper until you can get one.

As a beginner, count your stitches to prevent your projects from becoming wavy and uneven.

Start off with good posture. Developing this habit early on will save you trouble in the future.

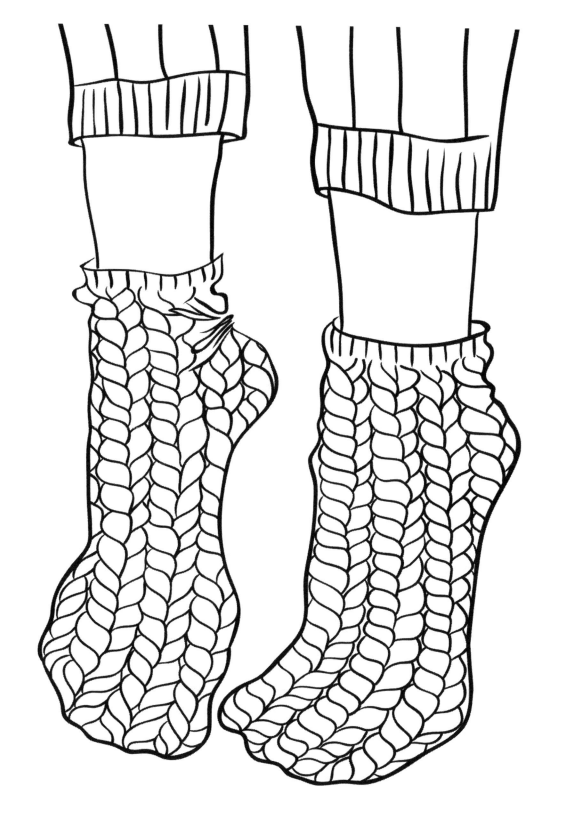

Master the knit and purl stitches.

Use wooden, bamboo. If you use metal needles take caution as they are more slippery and the reflection causes issues with some knitters.

Push the right needle through the next stitch. Go beyond the tapering on the needle and onto the wider portion.

Move from right to left.

For clean, crisp rows when adding a new color. Knit the entire row with the new color and continue with the ribbing.

Avoid tight stitches, don't knit at the very tip of the needle

It's not a race. You'll enjoy the journey much more if you relax and take your time.

Involve the whole family. Teach your children how to finger crochet so they can participate with you.

When resuming after a break, try not to tug on the yarn. If you do, bring the yarn down and towards your body.

Protect your investment by using the proper storage for your supplies. Dusty yarn is a big headache.

No shortcuts with yarn. Yarn weight plays a huge role in the size and appearance a finished project. Using a different weight out of convenience may have unintended consequences.

Use the tail to determine which side you are knitting on.

Don't forget to take breaks. Your hands and arms will thank you for it.

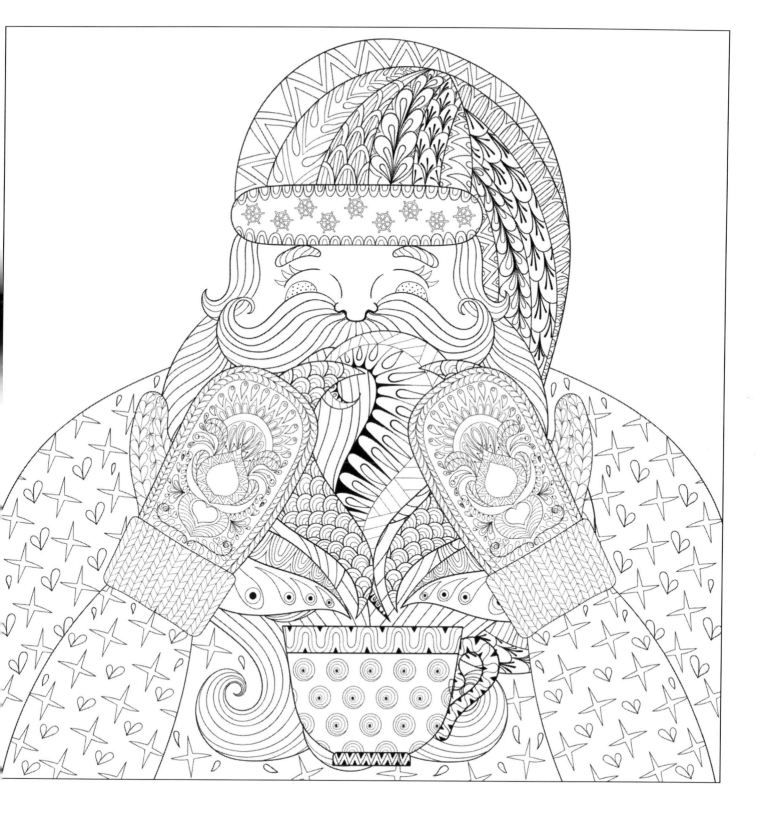

When choosing a crochet needle, select a hook size of either H or I. These work for most basic projects as they provide a good balance between usability and handling.

Don't neglect on gauge swatches. Most stitch tighter at the ends than in the middle. Use swatches to make sure you're size comes out correct.

Don't pull on yarn.

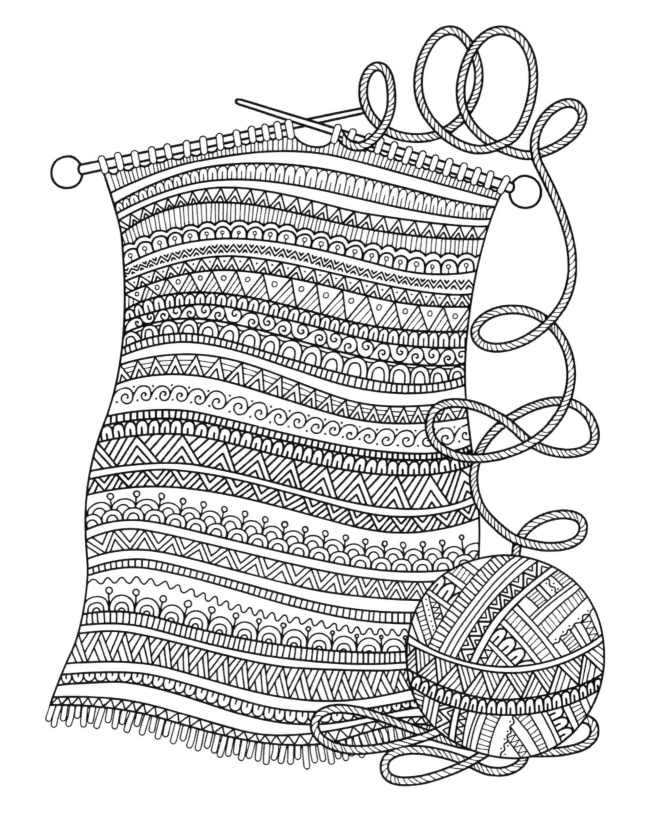

Final results a little lopsided? Add a border to give a nice finished look.

Do your projects look different when looking at them from behind? Make sure you're using both the front and back loops while stitching.

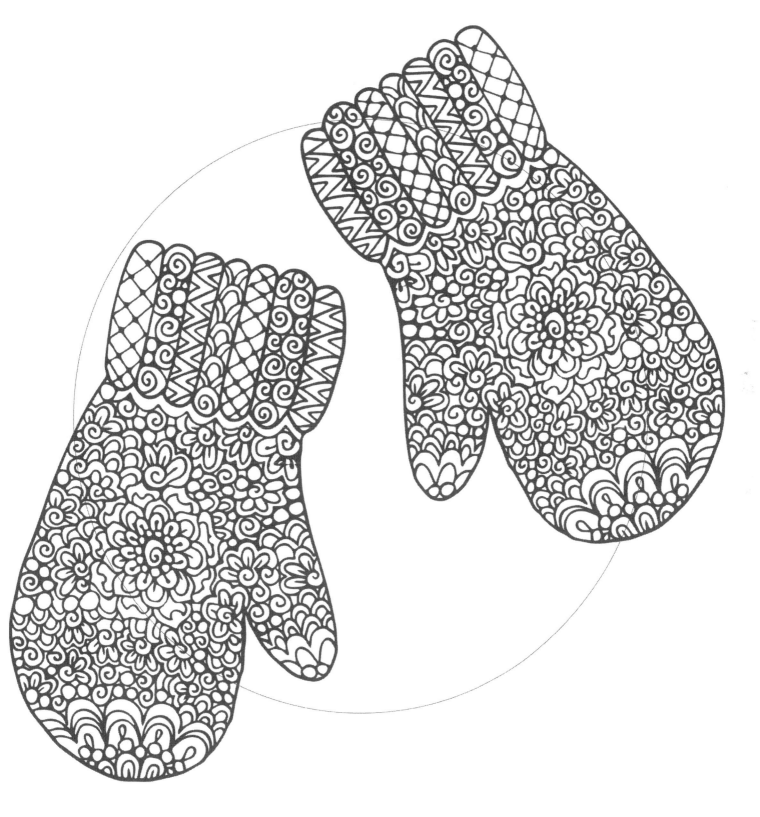

Soften inexpensive yarn by putting in a pillow case and washing with fabric softener or vinegar.

To prevent balls of yarn from falling or rolling away, keep them in an empty hand/diaper wipe container and pull the yarn through the hole.

Hide your tails by weaving them through your finished project.

Make use of scraps and ends by making pom poms, bracelets, or using as stuffing for pillows and stuffed animals.

To correct twisted stitches, simply knit into the back loop.

When first learning, stick with basic and inexpensive yarn.

Make needles easier to hold by adding tape and rubber pencil grips to them.

If fraying is making it difficult to thread a needle, dip the end in clear nail polish and twist tight while drying.

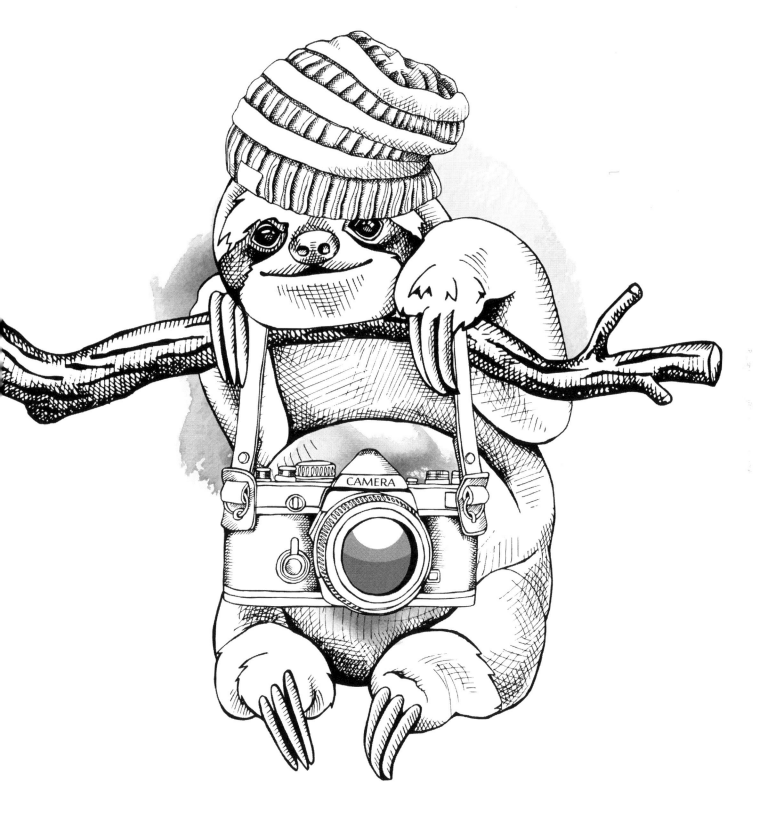

Organize your materials. Especially your needles, so you can swap needles quickly and ensure correct tension and work ribbing.

When using multiple colors of yarn, make sure they have the same thickness.

Yarn stretches and sags with time and use. Minimize this by using one of the various blocking techniques at the end of your project.

Tight hands make tight stitches. Relax, it's supposed to be fun.

Other amazing adult coloring books available on Amazon.com:

*Head Over Heels
An Adult Coloring Book for
Fashionistas and Shopaholics*

*Mandalas and More
Adult Coloring Book*

*The Dreamcatcher & Mandala
Coloring Book for Relaxation and
Stress Relief*

*The Adult Coloring Book of
Amazing Faces and Abstract Art*

RWSquaredMedia.Wordpress.com

Test Page

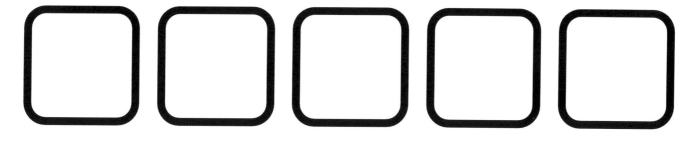

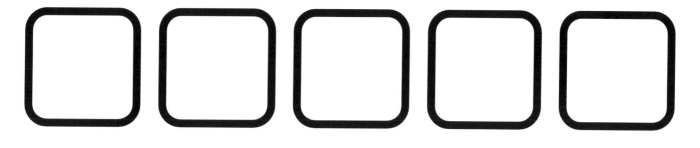

57581316R00049

Made in the USA
Middletown, DE
18 December 2017